Washed and Dried

poems by

Nancy Swanson

Finishing Line Press
Georgetown, Kentucky

Washed and Dried

ACKNOWLEDGMENTS

Many thanks to the following journals for publishing poems included in this
chapbook:

Broad River Review: "I Know Water"
Chattahoochee Review: "Lighthouse"
The Reach of Song: "Summer Day"
The South Carolina Review: "River Trails"
Kakalak: "Savannah River Basin"
Connecticut River Review: "Small Change"
North Carolina Literary Review: "Deep Woods"

"Ghost House" was a finalist for the Patricia Dobler Award and published on
the Madwomen in the Attic Website of Carlow University

Publisher: Leah Huete de Maines
Editor: Christen Kincaid
Cover Art: Nancy Swanson
Author Photo: Ben Rankin
Cover Design: Elizabeth Maines McCleavy

Order online: www.finishinglinepress.com
also available on amazon.com

Author inquiries and mail orders:
Finishing Line Press
PO Box 1626
Georgetown, Kentucky 40324
USA

Contents

Fort Myers Beach

The elderly are heat seekers, moving south for their golden years
in Florida. They begin with four bedrooms, a pool for grandkids,
then move to a pastel cinderblock house with a small yard.

Grandpa cultivates grapefruit. Each morning he picks one,
sprinkles the red flesh with sugar, digs out one tiny triangle
at a time with a notched spoon, and methodically eats breakfast.

He greets us as we wake in waves and find cereal, pecan rolls,
powdered sugar donuts from a white bag. My sister washes dishes,
trims Mama's hair, wipes down walls while we collect towels
and beach toys, fill a cooler, assemble the children in overheated
cars while traffic builds. Ocean, sand, tacky shops, the open-air bar,
our day at the beach are worth the wait.

Hurricane Ian took that beach on September 28, 2022,
including the seaside joint where my sister and I
posed on plastic chairs. And April 20, 2023,
COVID swept her, too, out to sea.

I Know Water

I have swum with jellyfish and dolphins
floated weightless in the arms of my love
shared the Pacific current with hump-backed whales

body surfed in an Atlantic wind-whipped to foam
dog paddled down rock-floored rivers
and waded tide pools digging for clams.

A child, I floated with new-cut grass
in a pond created by Hazel on her journey
from the ocean, 317 miles away.

After the yard drained and grew prickly
I lay beneath the arc of tepid sprinklers.
Today I bow my head for baptism

by the thirteenth hurricane of the season
and remember our neighbor's pool
cement on the bottom, polished tile up the sides.

And the deep end, populated by sun rays
that penetrated the clarity in solid shafts of yellow
while I descended, lingering

beneath clouds until I had to push upward
to gulp a breath of air and descend again.
On weekends, grownups took over

while I trained as waterside bartender, watching
too much to drink wash across the
flat, over-chlorinated pool.

One tipsy summer evening, the neighbor proclaimed
that all dogs could swim and threw my boxer Jerry
in the deep end, where he sank to the bottom

without protest until Daddy raised him up
thrashing from the clear blue spell
the deep, quiet solitude of water.

King's Highway
Near Kapoho Bay, Maui

As we approach, he offers his back, pretending
to examine chains and locks on the gate across
a gravel road to his invisible home, above.
We stop, waiting until he turns to the road,
crevices on his dark face unmoved by our smiles.
>We want to hike the old King's Highway.
>Do you know how to get there?

People die there. And it takes weeks
to find them. Don't go.

Heedless, we follow rented jeeps and convertibles
through tropical foliage and jagged hills,
pass a roadside stand for elk burgers,
pull off to squint against the merciless Pacific
and descend to a faint track
>across fingers of lava from 1790
>eroded into rolling lava rock.

People die there. And it takes weeks
to find them. Don't go.

Careless in our flip flops, we wander aimlessly
without water, follow maps into blind gulches,
lose the thread that disappears
>beneath cairns of sharp red and gray stone,
>into caves claimed by the homeless,
>under a rising sea,

seeking King Pi'ilani's Highway,
Maui's lost secret, treasured dream.

Lighthouse
St. Augustine, Florida

Thrust against a storybook-blue sky
And guarding a tidy, red-roofed cube,
This is surely a different lighthouse
Than the one we tried to visit once,
Or maybe it's the other side,
Not our first sighting down a deserted lane,
Above and beyond a driveway so shaded and quiet
That grass grew between two ruts.

I was sure we could tiptoe past a ghostly cottage
And through the yard to the back door.
But brambles blocked us
So completely we retreated
With a promise to come back another day.

Inside every lighthouse are winding stairs,
A darkened, hollow echo,
Windows with a slice of shore and breakers.
The top narrows so you can slide
Your hands along gray walls
As you take the last turns
Into sunlight and air, held only by red rails,
And stand there against the wind
Knowing the descent will drop you
Back to earth, where your breath
Isn't snatched away by high winds.

I didn't mind the broken promise:
This bookmark bought on a quiet afternoon
Is the same safe recollection as yours,
Probably settled by now to the bottom
Of your cluttered backpack.

Summer Day

When I empty this memory from 1955 like loose change
on the table, what tumbles out is two chubby sisters
wearing identical red bathing suits.

We have ridden to Hidden Valley Country Club
in the back seat of a big black car, buffeted
by hot wind laced with the smell of dry summer grass.

Mama takes our picture in the pool and returns to a lawn chair
with striped webbing that will unravel by Labor Day.
I watch her pick flakes of Lucky Strike from her tongue
and swing one long leg as she leafs through a magazine,
elegant in her yellow, two-piece bathing suit.

I don't remember others, even Daddy or Robert,
only Vince Little, whose hand pulled me to sunlight
when the bottom of the pool disappeared,
the edge became as indistinct and far away
as the people I would someday love.

The Winter It Snowed Six Feet

Joanne never let me borrow her clothes, so I waited,
    hoping she would pass them down.

She wore out the cherry dress with a wide collar and
    plastic belt, bought for Daddy's 43rd birthday.

But, when I was twelve she gave me the red and white
    pleated skirt--in the middle of a snowstorm.

This is a summer skirt, she warned. Weeks later I wear it
    under my winter coat the first day back to school.

And, while we stand at the bus stop beside the newly
    cleared road, one lacy flake falls.

More follow. When white covers the ground, we drop
    our books to make muddy snowballs.

As we leave wet clothes at the door, winter sets in to deliver
    another long holiday, but the skirt I wore just once
    becomes memory.

Spring Break

Round-eyed, solemn children open windows to
soft moss, leafy trails, profound water falling
into shallow pools, release from lectures, naps,
fractions and spelling.

Stifling giggles, shuffling and strutting, they flee,
slapping branches over their heads, and race to
creek beds. Ankle deep, they engineer dams of
sticks, mud, and smooth rocks.

Empty wooden desks in a lifeless, stuffy room
greet the teacher, clutching papers she has stained
purple down the hall. For an hour she wrings her
hands, paces the rows.

Found at last, lazily spread on warm rocks, or
draped on limbs with pocketed treasures—mushrooms,
pine cones, lichens, violets— kids line up and
return for snack time.

Made to copy letters from the chalkboard that
afternoon, hems of their pants wet, shades closed, they
dream of forest paths in deep shade, flowing streams,
escaping again.

River Trails

i

Standing in the cold water of the Chattooga,
The blue chips of his eyes
Hidden deep in his eighty years,
My great grandfather gave me a knife
That I keep in the table beside my bed.

Sometimes, hunting for a pencil,
Tape, a paper clip, an unpaid bill,
My fingers graze it,
Lying hard where time has shuffled
Its heaviness to a back corner.

The blade folds inside smooth wood,
The edge as keen after thirty winters
As his words: *Remember*
A good knife is like a good man:
Worth keeping a lifetime.

ii

On flat stones that almost broke the surface
We tiptoed to a boulder so huge
You had to reach over
And pull me up the rounded side.
We ate oranges
And watched the peels catch in eddies
Before tumbling downstream.

When a fisherman waded by
We regarded him silently from our dome,
Waiting for him to get around a bend
To take off our shirts
And lie, fingertips touching, collecting the warmth.

iii
Water drips from the roof
Of my gray tent
Driving me outside
Where grass crackles underfoot
And the fire has gone out.

Late fall leaves, sepia colored
Like old photographs,
Cushion my hiking boots
As I crouch to find a sweat shirt
In my overstuffed backpack.

Above the highest clouds
Raindrops float in thin air
And collect in piles of white mist
That the sun will eat
By the time I find the trail again.

Savannah River Basin

In summer the lakes sink in on themselves
leaving a red gash of bank and shallow pools
to collect mosquitoes and green film.

They sense the ebb, a sucking eddy
around gnarled and rusty barbed wire,
sodden stumps, abandoned tractors,
and bury in their cool depths cabins
and barns where carp and bass rest,
fins barely moving, in dark corners.

In drought, old bridges rise from the river
flooded half a century ago, and teenagers
paddle canoes over to wave from a road
erected before their grandfathers' war.

Further out, pine trees infested with beetles die,
fields beside the highway turn from yellow to brown,
and South Carolina simmers in heat that soaks humidity
from every puddle and stream to feed man's lakes
strung like pearls along three hundred miles of river.

July Rain

A dog in a mud puddle by the side of the road,
tongue hanging out like a fat red worm,
and this child, my son,
      watch clouds approach the firecracker stand
      closed for the afternoon storm.

It will continue for an hour, the storm,
erasing the accumulated sludge of traffic exhaust
and Carolina clay from the cinderblock building
as hard rain slides down the windshield in rapids
on this afternoon when we buy no fireworks,
      an afternoon when we wait together silently,
      not caring if the rain ever stops falling.

Leaving the Storm

Sloughing through invisible
puddles, lost in torrents, I escaped
under black clouds unburdening rain

worried that the carton of eggs
on the kitchen counter by the window
would ripen and smell

that the dishwasher was full and unstarted
and would stay that way as long
as I moved on

that when I had to stop for gas
in three or four hundred miles
I would remember my credit card

was in the pocket of jeans shuffled
under the bed or on the dresser cluttered
with receipts and unpaired earrings.

But I could not turn around
or even stop to look, as I
outdistanced familiar roads

and drove, squinting, straight
into clouds ahead glowing with light.

Aloha Miracles

Oahu already visible, we accelerate over palms, sand, a vast and
featureless Pacific, rising along the one uninhabited rocky shore
of Maui. It's a half hour flight with a family of seven Hawaiians
speaking pidgin. We eat breakfast in the terminal café before my
X-rays and report to a receptionist who remembers the Mexican
restaurant and bad water of her home, 2800 miles away, but just
minutes from the house we have rented in South Carolina.

Surrounded by wheelchairs pushed by children and spouses,
patients with legs missing, braces and bandages, the stoicism
of sustained pain, my voyage across the room is embarrassingly
easy. I got extra credit for twisting the arm with a plate and 16
screws behind my back, but the doctor deserved an A+.

Walking to the next appointment, we share two miles of windy,
palm-lined streets with the homeless: a teenager unconscious
against a building, his clothes caked with mud, dozens pushing
overfilled grocery carts, a hundred gathered in a park where
police won't disturb their rest nor their worldly possessions
in Banyan trees.

Politely, we look the other way to study moving sculptures across
the highway, taking pictures between stoplights. Just past the
Goodwill Store and Safeway we sip hot tea in a stainless lobby
but still arrive half an hour early. The oncologist delivers
good news.

We wait half an hour for a cab, watching kids on their way home
from school, mothers with babies, and a ninety-pound woman
who darts between cars to rescue her grocery cart. She ignores
cheers when she emerges, pushing her treasures. The cabbie talks
story: the rupture of two disks lifting a 400-pound ice addict,
an upcoming move to Las Vegas, his son at UNLV, and then
gives us a free ride to the airport.

Deposited among the frantically waving fronds of the Kahului airport, we recover our car and head upcountry through cane fields. We drive under a Maui rainbow, past Jacaranda trees covered in purple blooms, to reach our ohana halfway up a volcano, almost at the end of our years in Hawaii, just before it was forever changed.

On the Beach

When the family went to Virginia Beach,
Daddy simmered under an umbrella,
        his feet covered by towels.

We stayed in a big hotel across the street from
the beach and shared a room with two double beds
        and a cot for my little brother.

The summer after my sister's wedding, they reserved
two rooms at Myrtle Beach: one for my parents
        another for my brother and me.

Our motel was brand new, erected between sprawling
houses owned by people with more money
        than anyone we knew.

The first night, Mom and Dad drank free Martinis
at the bar and called friends while we ordered
        anything we wanted at the restaurant.

Robert got shrimp cocktail and chocolate pudding.
Whatever I ordered has disappeared along with
        a million other meals.

The word spread, carloads of parents with children
arrived the next day for free martinis, and the
        kids built a campfire on the beach.

It was my first time to watch waves lit by the moon,
        and fall under the transcendental
            spell of the ocean at night.

Graduation Day

I'm in the passenger seat, feet out the window,
       on the dappled two-lane road
       to the rest of my life.
I've skipped marching to leave early for a week
       in a ramshackle house two blocks
       from the beach.
My food contribution, yellow metal cans
       of Gordon's Potato Chips,
       takes up most of the back seat.

Each day we pack coolers and beach bags,
       grab portable radios, and head for
       the open-air donut shop.
By eleven, we're on the beach. We slather
       on Coppertone or baby oil mixed
       with iodine, and stay until we can't
       stand it anymore.
The walk back, always too hot, too long, ends
       in a flurry of girls with too few showers
       and no air conditioning.
At sunset we leave again, carrying fake ID's,
       for an outdoor bar with beer cans
       piled in the corners and the club
       that introduced the Tams.

Teachers in Vernazza

All the below the train station have green shutters.
We descend to discover Nicolina holding a sign
CAMERE ECONOMICHE and follow her stilettoes
up one hundred and twelve steps to the rental.

While the others inspect and bargain, I lug suitcases
large and heavy as boulders up more steps to find
the aqua Mediterranean trapped between mountains.
Rows of olive trees, leaning downhill, climb one slope;
a castle-become-hotel perches on top of the other. I decide
to honeymoon there if I get married again.

We gather chairs around a plastic-draped table pushed
against the only window, pour red wine, and blow smoke
into the alley, exclaiming over hand-painted ceramic tiles,
a marble block once used to roll pasta, photos of five cities
connected by walking trails.

Four single beds line the walls, one a child's with shiny red
metal head and foot boards. Damp sheets flutter across the alley
in swaths of light, and a dog seated at the dinner table stares
back at us from the other side. Later we will meet his master,
Christian. He lingers at tables of American women, knowing
they will leave an extra euro for the handsome young waiter
who speaks good English.

While darkness moves toward the sea, we listen to the clatter
of dishes and conversations on porches, cool under ivy-covered
lattices. Bells mark the hour, as they have for generations.

Our room must have been a home in this city of stone, the child
waking early to an empty plaza, sunrise stretched across
timeless waters where his father and uncles raise up
slick, salty calamari for tourists.

The first night I watch the faded globe beside his bed,
lit by moonlight, turn silently, almost imperceptibly,
on its brass stand until I fall asleep.

Dam Park Holiday

Orange and red townhouses along streets
with separate lanes for pedestrians, bikes,
and tiny cars line the Grachtengordel.

Queens from the nine museums wave from
boats like homecoming contestants
in the World's Largest Gay Parade.

Tourists flock to the red-light district to gawk
at the whores, and coffee shops sell chocolates
to children on the way to school.

All languages are spoken, all people are accepted,
no drugs are illegal, no bicycles are stolen, and flyers
with stick-figure drawings of safe sex are freely distributed.

Ah Amsterdam! Where friends sit on a stone wall
to sightsee and smoke a $7 triangular joint, leaving
half behind while we can still find the Indian restaurant.

Desert Dream

I live in a white two-story house with
no front porch and one scraggly
tree in the side yard. The McCoys
next door sometimes let us play
in the shade under their army of trees.

I wear pink glasses to correct my
wandering eye but they have been put
aside before bedtime. I can see perfectly
without them. I can even see sounds
from the living room bounce against
the foot of my bed because I want
to watch TV with my parents and big sister.

I am not afraid when the dream comes back:
me walking on hot white sand under a radiant,
throbbing sun, my destination a dark building
taller than it is wide. A sweet, dry odor permeates
the air. When a long shadow slides between
me and the light, a door opens and I wake.

The dream, soundless but endlessly
repeated through childhood, is the
secret I reveal now that I recognize
the sun, the odor, the shadow.

Small Change

In the back seat of our rented Mustang Convertible,
looking even smaller than 86 pounds,
she huddles into her white sweater,
a Christmas gift the year Ronald Reagan was elected.

My sister smiles at me from the driver's seat,
celebrating the bribe that pried Mama,
surrounded by relics of a lifetime,
from the recliner with a view of the asphalt parking lot.

She has no memory of 52 years with Daddy,
seven grandchildren, our husbands and names,
or her extended love affair with Lucky Strikes,
a relief to caretakers who push patients to the smoking garden.

But the offer of a beer from two middle-aged women
with familiar faces tucked her behind me, shivering
in the eighty-degree Florida breeze, reading signs:
Stop, McDonald's, Whiskey Creek Road, Four Miles to Ft. Myers.

Having looked at the morning paper, solved the jumble
and dropped it in her lap, she is happy to sip Budweiser
between crumbling front teeth she insists don't hurt
and talk about the sister she hasn't spoken to for sixty years.

And her beloved father, whose heart broke with the Depression.
We do know her, the four-year-old who taught herself to read,
graduated at 15, won every card game she ever played,
there, underneath the tarnish, as bright as a new, 1918 penny.

Ghost House

Although I do not know her
name I see a woman on her knees
planting hostas in the naked clay
of her new front yard

I discover her lilac wallpaper
beneath curtain brackets and
faded roses on the dark back wall
of the bathroom cabinet

The cat hair in the ducts and
under the refrigerator, buried in
the carpets, belongs to another
more recent ghost

I store her mail in a kitchen
drawer with yellowed papers
for replaced appliances and keys
that no longer work

Content to live with the women
if not their felines, I pick daffodils
in overgrown gardens marked
by mossy concrete blocks

Inside, they wrap me in their
faint, familiar scent as I wander
my twilight home

Watercolor

Spider webs fill the space between
parallel power lines dripping mist,
        their geometry visible from the road
                beside a pasture.

You could pull off to look
if the citified farmer had not
        built a fence which you cannot see
                but know is there.

You know a curve is there too
and a stop sign and birds singing
        to announce their presence in trees
                draped with fog.

Your mother kept flowered teacups
you might have treasured on a whatnot
        you dusted each Saturday morning,
                cups and whatnot now long gone.

But, like spider webs, fence, and birds,
        they do not matter.
The visible world is, after all, merely visible—
what you can remember, imagine, pass on
        but never own.

Cemetery Stanzas

i

I lead my class, with their notebooks and reluctance,
to a graveyard overlooking the Clemson football stadium.
Children, marked by stones with hand-carved names
and dates, rest with the infant grandson of John C. Calhoun,
his slaves in unmarked graves, and Coach Frank Howard.
All must sense trees burrowing into the niches, footfalls
of students on their way to parking, the roars of orange and
white faithful who gather each glorious fall, maybe even
a young body who lies across them, listening.

ii

Interstate 26 passes near an isolated graveyard
where we steal an hour before we are due home.
It is the first time we touch. You present me
with flowers plucked from a stone, and five years later,
with a smooth, white anniversary pebble.

iii

Cemetery Trail passes though the McCall burial site,
dug and filled and tended for two hundred years
before cars followed Highway 276 to the Parkway.
Now it is deserted except for hikers on a two-mile
moderate and those seeking a yellow-topped geocache
considerately located beyond the stones. Weather
and time have erased the names and dates.

iv

Mama, swallowed by a white sweater, sits in a folding
chair set before our father's urn, holding her purse
to her chest. Feet primly crossed at the ankles,
she poses, unaware that we will miss her exit four years later,
escape a speeding ticket because her ashes are in the back seat,
and regather, orphans, on the same green field.

v

The drugs took him a month before their first anniversary. Because he always wanted to be a tree, she had him buried, whole, at the foot of a giant live oak. The first Valentine's Day, she slept between the branches and him until dawn.

Deep Woods

As fall's first leaves float toward earth, I descend to the river,
following steps traced in dust, buried by mud, beneath
flat stones, and walk where wildlife paused to drink
before Columbus found the new world, already ancient.

Danger lies everywhere: the bright snake immobile and invisible
on the path, makeshift ladders that tremble underfoot, a brown
bear leading cubs to a crevice with liquid sliding down the walls,
a stumble, a wrong turn, a night without human comfort.

Worst, the insidious three-headed poison ivy, overgrown,
reaching from trailside, suspended from overhead branches.
I've lost my gloves, and push hands already contaminated
into pockets while I close my eyes and try to regain balance.

I stay an eternity, growing cold, remembering a vine-wrapped
child in a fort high enough to see home, my mother drinking
wine as she sets the table, the circle of light at the back door,
a tub of hot water that spreads the poison.

Although I simmered and bubbled for weeks,
I find no scar except the fear that sends me forward,
for there is nowhere else to go.

Nancy Swanson treasured her thirty-plus years in middle school, high school, tech school, and university classrooms, more than half in a small high school in South Carolina. When she arrived, writing was five paragraph essays, an occasional literary analysis, and term papers with footnotes and bibliographies. She was delighted to see this curriculum become extinct.

Her experiences with the Humanities Council, the South Carolina Governor's School for the Arts, Clemson University's Creative Writing Program, and the National Writing Project allowed her to help change come to the school, which created a variety of creative writing electives. Meanwhile she was writing with her students.

She thought of herself as a teacher who writes until she retired and became a poet. She spent some poems on the family and friends, and many on the past. However, as an avid hiker and backpacker, her primary focus has become the natural world, now so grievously threatened.